Pam Pats, Sam Taps!

By Debbie Croft

T0360125

It is Pam.

Pam sits at the pit.

Pat, pat, pat!

It is Sam.

Sit at the pit, Sam!

Sam sat at the pit.

Sam and Pam sat
at the pit.

CHECKING FOR MEANING

1. Who sat at the sandpit at the start of the story? *(Literal)*

2. Who sat at the sandpit at the end of the story? *(Literal)*

3. Why do you think Sam helped Pam build the sandcastle? *(Inferential)*

EXTENDING VOCABULARY

sits	Look at the word *sits*. What is the base of the word? What letter has been added to the base to make *sits*?
pat	Look at the word *pat*. What do Pam and Sam pat the sandcastle with? What other tools can you use to help make a sandcastle?
Sam	Look at the word *Sam*. What sounds are in this word? Can you find other words in the book that start with the same sound? What other words do you know that start with *s*?

MOVING BEYOND THE TEXT

1. What else can you do with sand besides making a sandcastle?

2. Use your senses to describe sand. What does it look like, feel like and sound like?

3. What are some different ways you can use a bucket?

4. What else would you like to do with your friends or family?

SPEED SOUNDS

Mm	Ss	Aa	Pp	Ii	Tt

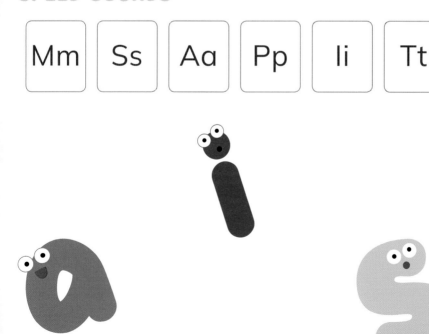

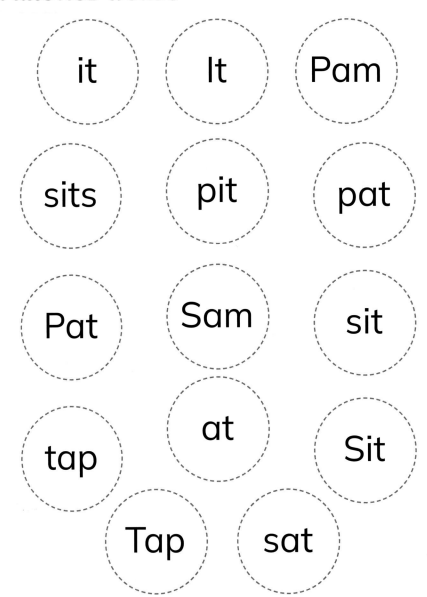

it

It

Pam

sits

pit

pat

Pat

Sam

sit

tap

at

Sit

Tap

sat